NEW EDITION — VOCAL SELECTIONS

WEST SIDE STORY

Based on a conception of Jerome Robbins

Music By
LEONARD BERNSTEIN

Lyrics By
STEPHEN SONDHEIM

Book By
ARTHUR LAURENTS

Entire original production
directed and choreographed by
Jerome Robbins

ISBN 978-0-634-04675-9

"West Side Story" is a registered trademark of The Leonard Bernstein Office, Inc.
The Name and Likeness of "Leonard Bernstein" is a registered trademark of Amberson Holdings LLC.
Used by permission

7777 W. Bluemound Rd. P.O. Box 13819 Milwaukee, WI 53213

For all works contained herein:
Unauthorized copying, arranging, adapting, recording or public performance is an infringement of copyright.
Infringers are liable under the law.

www.leonardbernstein.com
www.boosey.com
www.halleonard.com

Front Cover photo: from The Theatre Collection
Museum of the City of New York
Photo: Ellen Darby – Graphic House

All photographs, from the original Broadway production, on pages 12-19 are from
The Theatre Collection
Museum of the City of New York

The reproduction of Leonard Bernstein's manuscripts from *West Side Story*
is courtesy of The Library of Congress

CONTENTS

21	**Jet Song**
26	**Something's Coming**
40	**Promenade**
42	**Cha-Cha**
35	**Maria**
44	**Tonight**
48	**America**
52	**Cool**
55	**One Hand, One Heart**
60	**I Feel Pretty**
64	**Somewhere**
67	**Gee, Officer Krupke**
74	**I Have a Love**

LEONARD BERNSTEIN

Leonard Bernstein was born in Lawrence, Massachusetts, on August 25, 1918. He took piano lessons as a boy and attended the Garrison and Boston Latin Schools. At Harvard University, he studied with Walter Piston, Edward Burlingame-Hill, and A. Tillman Merritt, among others. Before graduating in 1939 he made an unofficial conducting debut with his own incidental music to *The Birds*, and directed and performed in Marc Blitzstein's *The Cradle Will Rock*. Subsequently, at the Curtis Institute of Music in Philadelphia, he studied piano with Isabella Vengerova, conducting with Fritz Reiner, and orchestration with Randall Thompson.

In 1940, he studied at the Boston Symphony Orchestra's newly created summer institute, Tanglewood, with the orchestra's conductor, Serge Koussevitzky. Bernstein later became Koussevitzky's conducting assistant. After making a sensational conducting debut with the New York Philharmonic in 1943, Bernstein became Music Director of the orchestra in 1958. From then until 1969 he led more concerts with the orchestra than any previous conductor. He subsequently held the lifetime title of Laureate Conductor, making frequent guest appearances with the orchestra. More than half of Bernstein's 400-plus recordings were made with the New York Philharmonic.

Beyond many distinguished achievements as a composer of concert works, Bernstein also wrote a one-act opera, *Trouble in Tahiti*, in 1952, and its sequel, the three-act opera, *A Quiet Place* in 1983. He collaborated with choreographer Jerome Robbins on three major ballets: *Fancy Free* (1944) and *Facsimile* (1946) for the American Ballet Theater; and *Dybbuk* (1975) for the New York City Ballet. He composed the score for the award-winning movie *On the Waterfront* (1954) and incidental music for the Broadway play *The Lark* (1955).

Bernstein contributed substantially to the Broadway musical stage. He collaborated with Betty Comden and Adolph Green on *On the Town* (1944) and *Wonderful Town* (1953). For *Peter Pan* (1950), he penned his own lyrics to songs and also composed incidental music. In collaboration with Richard Wilbur and Lillian Hellman and others he wrote *Candide* (1956). Other versions of *Candide* were written in association with Hugh Wheeler, Stephen Sondheim, et al. In 1957, he again collaborated with Jerome Robbins, Stephen Sondheim, and Arthur Laurents, on the landmark musical *West Side Story*, also made into the Academy Award-winning film. In 1976 Bernstein and Alan Jay Lerner wrote *1600 Pennsylvania Avenue*.

Bernstein received many honors. He was elected in 1981 to the American Academy of Arts and Letters, which gave him its Gold Medal. The National Fellowship Award in 1985 applauded his life-long support of humanitarian causes. He received the MacDowell Colony's Gold Medal; medals from the Beethoven Society and the Mahler Gesellschaft; the Handel Medallion, New York City's highest honor for the arts; a Tony award (1969) for Distinguished Achievement in the Theater; and dozens of honorary degrees and awards from colleges and universities. He was presented ceremonial keys to the cities of Oslo, Vienna, Bersheeva and the village Bernstein, Austria, among others. National honors came from Italy, Israel, Mexico, Denmark, Germany (the Great Merit Cross), and France (Chevalier, Officer and Commandeur of the Legion d'Honneur). He received the Kennedy Center Honors in 1980.

Bernstein was the father of three children—Jamie, Alexander, and Nina—and enjoyed the arrival of his first two grandchildren, Franscisca and Evan. Leonard Bernstein died on October 14, 1990.

STEPHEN SONDHEIM

Stephen Sondheim wrote the music and lyrics for *A Funny Thing Happened on the Way to the Forum* (1962), *Anyone Can Whistle* (1964), *Company* (1970), *Follies* (1971), *A Little Night Music* (1973), *The Frogs* (1974), *Pacific Overtures* (1976), *Sweeney Todd* (1979), *Merrily We Roll Along* (1981), *Sunday in the Park with George* (1984), *Into the Woods* (1987), *Assassins* (1991), *Passion* (1994) and *Bounce* (2003), as well as lyrics for *West Side Story* (1957), *Gypsy* (1959), *Do I Hear a Waltz?* (1965) and additional lyrics for *Candide* (1973). *Side By Side By Sondheim* (1976), *Marry Me a Little* (1981), *You're Gonna Love Tomorrow* (1983), *Putting It Together* (1993/1999) and *Moving On* (2001) are anthologies of his work as composer and lyricist. For films, he composed the scores of *Stavisky* (1974) and co-composed *Reds* (1981) as well as songs for *Dick Tracy* (1990). He also wrote the songs for the television production "Evening Primrose" (1966), co-authored the film *The Last of Sheila* (1973) and the play *Getting Away with Murder* (1996) and provided incidental music for the plays *The Girls of Summer* (1956), *Invitation to a March* (1961), *Twigs* (1971) and *The Enclave* (1973). *Saturday Night* (1954), his first professional musical, finally had its New York premiere in 1999. Mr. Sondheim has received the Tony Award for Best Score/Music/Lyrics for *Company, Follies, A Little Night Music, Into the Woods* and *Passion*, all of which won the New York Drama Circle Award for Outstanding/Best Musical, as did *Pacific Overtures* and *Sunday in the Park with George*. In total, his works have accumulated more than sixty individual and collaborative Tony Awards. "Sooner Or Later" from the film *Dick Tracy* won the 1999 Academy Award for Best Song. Mr. Sondheim received the Pulitzer Prize for Drama in 1984 for *Sunday in the Park with George*. In 1983 he was elected to the American Academy of Arts and Letters, which awarded him with the Gold Medal for Music in 2006. In 1990 he was appointed the first Visiting Professor of Contemporary Theatre at Oxford University and was the recipient of a Lifetime Achievement Award in the 1993 Kennedy Center Honors. Mr. Sondheim is on the Council of the Dramatists Guild, the national association of playwrights, composers and lyricists, having served as its President from 1973 to 1981. In 1981 he founded Young Playwrights Inc. to develop and promote the work of American playwrights aged 18 years and younger. (For information, write to Artistic@Youngplaywrights.org.)

Facsimile from the composer's manuscript of "Maria."

Facsimile from the composer's manuscript of "Something's Coming."

WEST SIDE STORY

Music: Leonard Bernstein
Lyrics: Stephen Sondheim
Book: Arthur Laurents

ORIGINAL BROADWAY PRODUCTION

Opened: September 26, 1957, Winter Garden Theatre, New York, for a run of 732 performances
Director: Jerome Robbins
Choreographer: Jerome Robbins

PRINCIPAL CAST

Maria – Carol Lawrence
Tony – Larry Kert
Anita – Chita Rivera
Bernardo – Ken Le Roy
Riff – Mickey Calin

SYNOPSIS

The show portrays a struggle for the streets of New York between two gangs. The Jets, a group of self-styled "American" teenagers, are led by cool Riff. The Sharks, who are Puerto Rican newcomers, are led by fiery Bernardo. This bitter rivalry has deep seeds in racial prejudice and cultural insensitivity. Riff decides he will challenge the Sharks to a rumble for dominance that night at the dance at a local gym. Riff convinces his former right hand man Tony to come to the dance to back him up. Tony has left the gang, going straight and working at Doc's drugstore. Amidst hot dancing at the gym, Bernardo's beautiful sister Maria, who had been brought from Puerto Rico to marry Chino, locks eyes with Tony and the two instantly fall in love. When Bernardo sees the two together, he quickly breaks them apart. At this moment Riff decides to put forward the challenge. The two rival gangs are to meet later that night to set the terms for the rumble. Tony steals away to see Maria on her fire escape. The gangs decide on a fair fight with no weapons. The next day, at the bridal shop where Maria works, after the two have committed themselves to one another, she convinces Tony to try to stop the fight. He arrives at the rumble to find Riff and Bernardo fighting with knives. He calls to Riff to spare Bernardo's life. When Riff is distracted by Tony, Bernardo kills Riff. Tony is enraged over his friend's death, and picks up his knife, stabs and kills Bernardo, and flees to meet Maria in her bedroom. Chino seeks to avenge Bernardo's death with a gun. Tony hides at Doc's drugstore. Maria sends Anita to bring a missive to Tony, but the Jets treat her cruelly, and instead she lies and says that Chino killed Maria. Tony is beside himself with grief, and runs from hiding, hoping Chino will kill him too. Instead, he finds Maria, and as they cross to embrace, Chino appears and shoots Tony dead. Maria runs to her fallen lover. She somberly watches as members of both the Jets and the Sharks carry off Tony's body.

BACKGROUND

The origins of *West Side Story* can be traced to early 1949. Jerome Robbins, who had conceived *On the Town*, approached Leonard Bernstein about a re-imagining and updating of Shakespeare's *Romeo and Juliet*. At the time, the story involved a Jewish boy and an Italian Catholic girl on New York's lower east side. Bernstein was interested, but had other commitments. In 1955 Robbins and Bernstein, along with Arthur Laurents, picked up the idea again, changing the players in the tale to reflect the mid-1950s mood and the issues over Puerto Rican immigration into the city. With the idea of rival gangs, *West Side Story* was off and running. A young Stephen Sondheim was brought on to write the lyrics. The authors tried to usher in a new kind of American drama with *West Side Story*, not quite opera, not quite Broadway, with a stronger emphasis on character and dance.

BROADWAY REVIVALS AND LONDON PRODUCTIONS

West Side Story was revived on Broadway twice, in 1964 at the City Center theatre for a run of 31 performances, and in 1980 at the Minskoff Theatre for a run of 333 performances. The 1964 revival starred Julia Migenes as Maria, and Don McKay as Tony, who also starred in the London premiere of 1958. The 1980 revival, directed by Robbins, starred Ken Marshall as Tony, choreographer Debbie Allen as Anita, and Josie De Guzman as Maria. The 1958 London production, which played at Her Majesty's Theatre for a run of 1,039 performances, also starred George Chakiris as Riff, Chita Rivera reprising her role as Anita, and Marlys Watters as Maria.

UNITED ARTISTS FILM VERSION (1961)

Directors: Robert Wise and Jerome Robbins
Screenplay: Ernest Lehman
Music: Leonard Bernstein
Lyrics: Stephen Sondheim

Robert Wise, who would later direct *The Sound of Music*, helped bring *West Side Story* to the screen in 1961, starring Natalie Wood (with the singing voice of Marni Nixon) as Maria, Richard Beymer as Tony (singing dubbed by Jim Bryant), and Rita Moreno as Anita. Almost all of the score was retained, but there were some major shifts in song and scene order for the film. The only person in the movie who had appeared on stage in *West Side Story* was George Chakiris (Bernardo) who had been in the London production as Riff. The movie took home 10 Oscars, including Best Picture.

RECORDINGS

1957 Original Broadway Cast, Sony 60724 • 1961 United Artists Film Soundtrack, Sony 48211 • Leonard Bernstein Conducts West Side Story (1985), Deutsche Grammophon 4152532GH2, *The Making of West Side Story* Deutsche Grammophon DVD 0734054 • 1993 UK Revival Highlights, Madecy Records 756 • 1997 Studio Cast (Complete Recording), Jay Records 1261

EXCERPTS FROM BERNSTEIN'S WEST SIDE LOG

In 1957, when West Side Story *premiered, Bernstein published a log of the show's genesis. This is his typescript:*

New York, 6 Jan., 1949
Jerry [Robbins] called today with a noble idea: a modern version of "Romeo and Juliet," set in slums at the coincidence of Easter-Passover celebrations. Feelings running high between Jews and Catholics. Former: Capulets, latter: Montagues. Juliet is Jewish. Friar Lawrence is a neighborhood druggist. Street brawls, double death—it all fits. But it's all much less important than the bigger idea of making a musical that tells a tragic story in musical comedy terms, using only musical comedy techniques, never falling into the "operatic" trap. Can it succeed? It hasn't yet in our country. I'm excited. If it can work—it's a first. Jerry suggests Arthur Laurents for the book. I don't know him, but I do know "Home of the Brave" at which I cried like a baby. He sounds just right.

New York, 10 Jan., 1949
Met Arthur L. at Jerry's tonight. Long talk about opera versus whatever this should be. Fascinating. We're going to have a stab at it.

Columbus, Ohio, 15 April, 1949
Just received draft of first four scenes. Much good stuff. But this is no way to work. Me on this long conducting tour, Arthur between New York and Hollywood. Maybe we'd better wait until I can find a continuous hunk of time to devote to the project. Obviously this show can't depend on stars, being about kids; and so it will have to live or die by the success of its collaborations; and this remote-control collaboration isn't right. Maybe they can find the right composer who isn't always skipping off to conduct somewhere. It's not fair to them or to the work.

New York, 7 June, 1955
Jerry hasn't given up. Six years of postponement are as nothing to him. I'm still excited too. So is Arthur. Maybe I can plan to give this year to "Romeo" – if "Candide" gets on in time.

Beverly Hills, 25 August, 1955
Had a fine long session with Arthur today, by the pool. (He's here for a movie; I'm conducting at the Hollywood Bowl.) We're fired again by the "Romeo" notion; only now we have abandoned the whole Jewish-Catholic premise as not very fresh, and have come up with what I think is going to be it: two teen-age gangs as the warring factions, one of them newly-arrived Puerto Ricans, the other self-styled "Americans." Suddenly it all springs to life. I hear rhythms and pulses, and—most of all—I can sort of feel the form.

New York, 6 Sept., 1955
Jerry loves our gang idea. A second solemn pact has been sworn. Here we go, God bless us!

New York, 14 Nov., 1955
A young lyricist named Stephen Sondheim came and sang us some of his songs today. What a talent! I think he's ideal for this project, as do we all. The collaboration grows.

New York, 17 March, 1956
"Candide" is on again; we plunge in next month. So again "Romeo" is postponed for a year. Maybe it's all for the best: by the time it emerges it ought to be deeply seasoned, cured, hung, aged in the wood. It's such a problematical work anyway that it should benefit by as much sitting-time as it can get. Chief problem: to tread the fine line between opera and Broadway, between realism and poetry, ballet and "just dancing," abstract and representational. Avoid being "messagy." The line is there, but it's very fine, and sometimes takes a lot of peering around to discern it.

New York, 1 Feb., 1957
"Candide" is on and gone; the Philharmonic has been conducted, back to "Romeo." From here on nothing shall disturb the project: whatever happens to interfere I shall cancel summarily. It's going too well now to let it drop again.

New York, 8 July, 1957
Rehearsals. Beautiful sketches for sets by Oliver [Smith]. Irene [Sharaff] showed us costume sketches: breathtaking. I can't believe it—forty kids are actually doing it up there on the stage! Forty kids singing five-part counterpoint who never sang before—and sounding like heaven. I guess we were right not to cast "singers": anything that sounded more professional would inevitably sound more experienced, and then the "kid" quality would be gone. A perfect example of a disadvantage turned into a virtue.

Washington, D.C., 20 Aug., 1957
The opening last night was just as we dreamed it. All the peering and agony and postponements and re-re-re-writing turn out to have been worth it. There's a work there; and whether it finally succeeds or not in Broadway terms, I am now convinced that what we dreamed all these years is possible; because there stands that tragic story, with a theme as profound as love versus hate, with all the theatrical risks of death and racial issues and young performers and "serious" music and complicated balletics—and it all added up for audience and critics. I laughed and cried as though I'd never seen or heard it before. And I guess that what made it come out right is that we all really collaborated; we were all writing the same show. Even the producers were after the same goals we had in mind. Not even a whisper about a happy ending has been heard. A rare thing on Broadway. I am proud and honored to be a part of it.

DRAMATISTS GUILD EXCERPT

In 1985, the authors of West Side Story *came together at a Dramatists Guild Landmark Symposium to discuss their work. Terrence McNally acted as Moderator. The transcript of the entire session was published in the Dramatists Guild Quarterly (Autumn 1985). In the following excerpts, Jerome Robbins and Leonard Bernstein discuss the origin of the show and the collaboration that produced it.*

TERRENCE McNALLY: It's hard to imagine what the musical theater would be like in 1985 without the efforts of the four gentlemen sitting here with me, the authors of *West Side Story*. In our theater community, they are held in great, great respect and much love. *West Side Story* is the one time these four extraordinary talents came together. I'd like to start with the germ of the idea, the first time somebody said, "Hey, there's a musical there," up through opening night in New York, in this case September 26, 1957, when *West Side Story* opened at the Winter Garden Theater.

JEROME ROBBINS: I don't remember the exact date—it was somewhere around 1949—a friend of mine was offered the role of Romeo. He said to me, "This part seems very passive, would you tell me what you think I should do with it." I tried to imagine it in terms of today. That clicked in, and I said to myself, "There's a wonderful idea here." So I wrote a very brief outline and started looking for a producer and collaborators who'd be interested. This was not easy. Producers were not at all interested in doing it. Arthur and Lenny were interested, but not in getting together to work on it at that time, so we put it away. Many years later, they were involved in another musical and asked me to join them. I was not interested in their musical, but I did manage to say, "How about Romeo and Juliet?" I won them back to the subject, and that started our collaboration.

McNALLY: Were Arthur and Lenny the first librettist and composer you approached?

ROBBINS: Oh, yes. During the long period we put the project aside, I wasn't actively seeking other collaborators, I thought these were the best people for the material. I stuck to trying to get these guys, and when they came back to me I had the bait to grab them…

McNALLY: Lenny, part of the West Side Story lore is that you intended to do the lyrics yourself. Is that true?

LEONARD BERNSTEIN: …Yes, when we began I had— madly—undertaken to do the lyrics as well as the music. In 1955, I was also working on another show, *Candide*, and then the *West Side Story* music turned out to be extraordinarily balletic—which I was very happy about—and turned out to be a tremendously greater amount of music than I had expected, ballet music, symphonic music, developmental music. For those two reasons, I realized that I couldn't do all that music, plus the lyrics, and do them well. Arthur mentioned that he'd heard a young fellow named Stephen Sondheim sing some of his songs at a party…I freaked out when Steve came in and sang his songs. From that moment to this, we've been loving colleagues and friends…

ROBBINS: I'd like to talk a little bit about that period, because it was one of the most exciting I've ever had in the theater: the period of the collaboration, when we were feeding each other all the time. We would meet wherever we could, depending on our schedules. Arthur would come in with a scene, the others would say they could do a song on this material, I'd supply, "How about if we did this as a dance?" There was this wonderful, mutual exchange going on. We can talk here about details, "I did this, I did that," but the essence of it was what we gave to each other, took from each other, yielded to each other, surrendered, reworked, put back together again, all of those things. It was a very important and extraordinary time. The collaboration was most fruitful during that digestive period. I say that because we got turned down so much, and for so many reasons, that we kept going back to the script, or rather our play, saying, "That didn't work, I wonder why not, what didn't they like, let's take a look at it again."

I remember Richard Rodger's contribution. We had a death scene for Maria—she was going to commit suicide or something, as in Shakespeare. He said, "She's dead already, after this all happens to her." So the walls we hit were helpful to us in a way, sending us back for another look. I'm glad we didn't get West Side Story on right away. Between the time we thought of it and finally did it, we did an immense amount of work on it.

BERNSTEIN: Amen to that. This was one of the most extraordinary collaborations of my life, perhaps the most, in that very sense of our nourishing one another. There was a generosity on everybody's part that I've rarely seen in the theater. For example, the song "Something's Coming" was a very late comer. We realized we needed a character-introduction kind of song for Tony. There was a marvelous introductory page in the script that Arthur had written, a kind of monologue, the essence of which became the lyric for the song. We raped Arthur's playwriting. I've never seen anyone so encouraging, let alone generous, urging us, "Yes, take it, take it, make it a song."

Reprinted from *The Dramatists Guild Quarterly* © 1985. All rights reserved.
With thanks to Terrence McNally and the Estate of Jerome Robbins.

The following pages contain photographs from the original Broadway Production

The creative team of *West Side Story*, 1957.

Left to Right:
**Stephen Sondheim (lyricist),
Arthur Laurents (book author),
Hal Prince (producer),
Leonard Bernstein (composer),
Jerome Robbins (director/choreographer);**
Seated: **Robert E. Griffith (producer).**

Photo: Friedman-Abeles

Arthur Laurents *(standing)* **and Jerome Robbins confer in rehearsal, while Carol Lawrence (Maria) and Larry Kert (Tony) listen.**

Photo: Friedman-Abeles

Leonard Bernstein in rehearsal with the cast, Carol Lawrence on the right *(in stripes)*, **with Chita Rivera standing behind Stephen Sondheim at the piano.**
Photo: Friedman-Abeles

Leonard Bernstein in rehearsal with the cast, with Carol Lawrence standing behind him; Chita Rivera's back is to the camera.

In rehearsal: Chita Rivera (Anita), center, Jerome Robbins on her right.

Photo: Friedman-Abeles

The cast in dance rehearsal.

Tony and Maria in the Balcony Scene ("Tonight").

Photo: Fred Fehl

The dance at the Gym.
Photo: Fred Fehl

Anita in the dance at the gym.
Photo: Fred Fehl

Larry Kert (Tony) and Carol Lawrence (Maria) in rehearsal.
Photo: Friedman-Abeles

The Jets dance in "Cool."
Photo: Fred Fehl

The Jets at the drugstore in "Cool."
Photo: Ellen Darby – Graphic House

"The Rumble."
Photo: Fred Fehl

"Gee, Officer Krupke."
Photo: Fred Fehl

Anita and Maria, "I Have a Love."
Photo: Fred Fehl

The Sharks

From the 1961 United Artists Motion Picture

JET SONG

Music by LEONARD BERNSTEIN
Lyrics by STEPHEN SONDHEIM

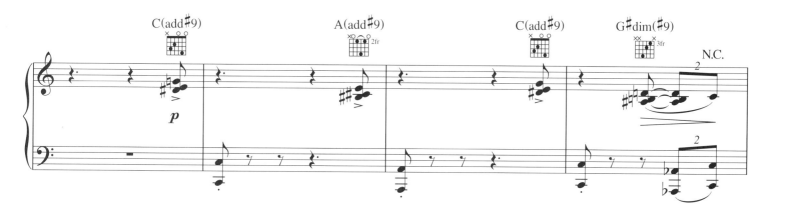

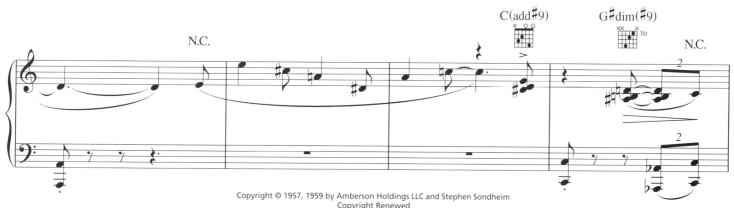

Copyright © 1957, 1959 by Amberson Holdings LLC and Stephen Sondheim
Copyright Renewed
This arrangement Copyright © 2007 by Amberson Holdings LLC and Stephen Sondheim
Leonard Bernstein Music Publishing Company LLC, Publisher
Boosey & Hawkes, Inc., Sole Agent
Copyright For All Countries   All Rights Reserved

22

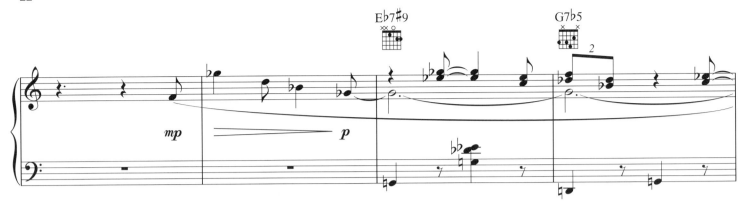
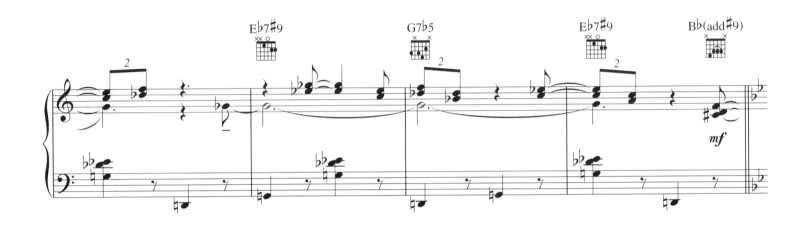
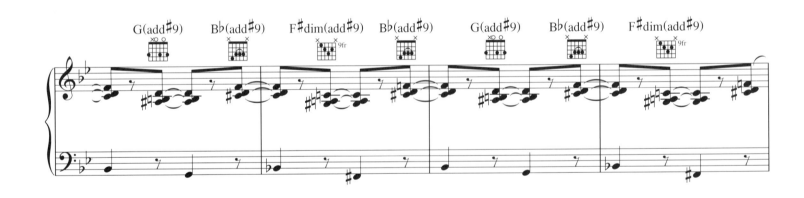

SOMETHING'S COMING

Music by LEONARD BERNSTEIN
Lyrics by STEPHEN SONDHEIM

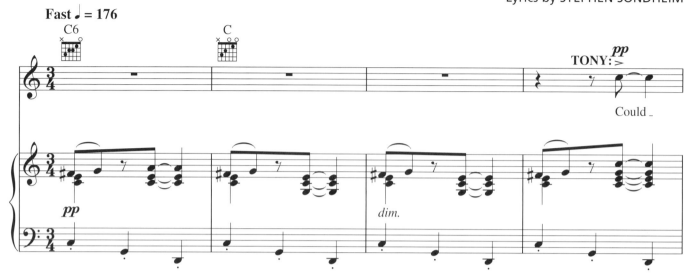
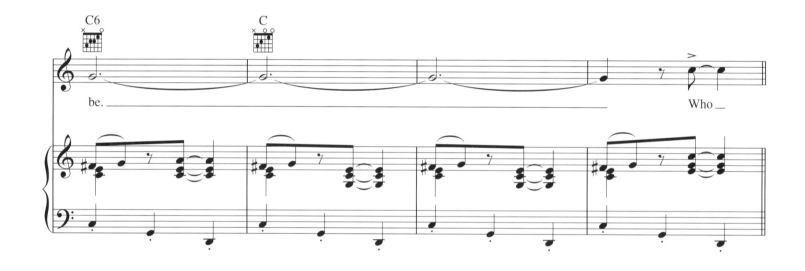
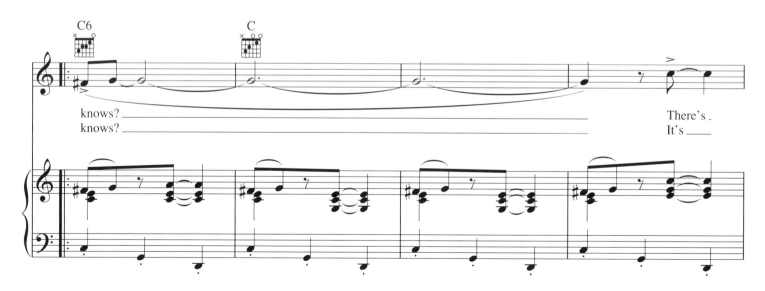

Copyright © 1957 by Amberson Holdings LLC and Stephen Sondheim
Copyright Renewed
This arrangement Copyright © 2007 by Amberson Holdings LLC and Stephen Sondheim
Leonard Bernstein Music Publishing Company LLC, Publisher
Boosey & Hawkes, Inc., Sole Agent
Copyright for All Countries. All Rights Reserved.

MARIA

Music by LEONARD BERNSTEIN
Lyrics by STEPHEN SONDHEIM

Copyright © 1957 by Amberson Holdings LLC and Stephen Sondheim
Copyright Renewed
This arrangement Copyright © 2007 by Amberson Holdings LLC and Stephen Sondheim
Leonard Bernstein Music Publishing Company LLC, Publisher
Boosey & Hawkes, Inc., Sole Agent
Copyright for All Countries. All Rights Reserved.

PROMENADE

Music by
LEONARD BERNSTEIN

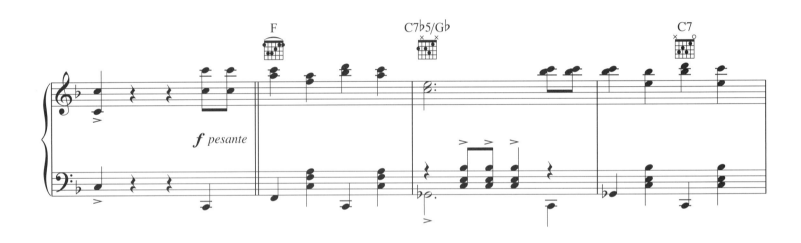
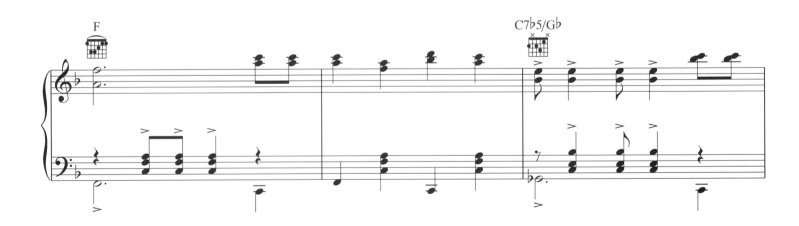

Copyright © 1957, 1959 by Amberson Holdings LLC and Stephen Sondheim
Copyright Renewed
This arrangement Copyright © 2007 by Amberson Holdings LLC and Stephen Sondheim
Leonard Bernstein Music Publishing Company LLC, Publisher
Boosey & Hawkes, Inc., Sole Agent
Copyright for All Countries. All Rights Reserved.

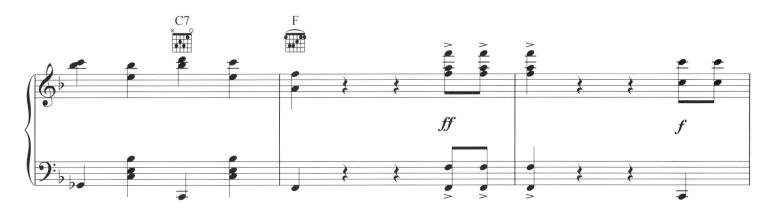
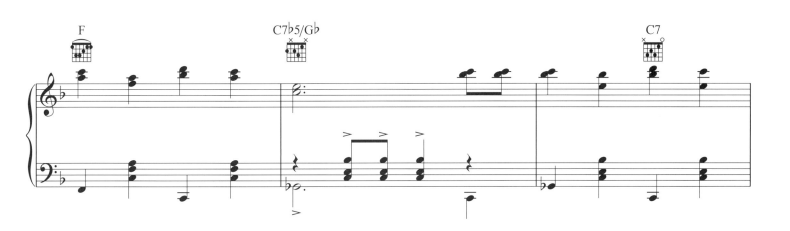
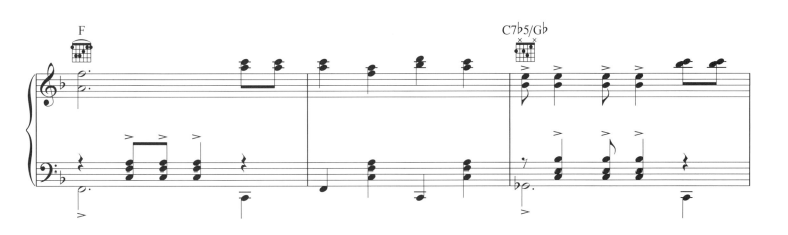
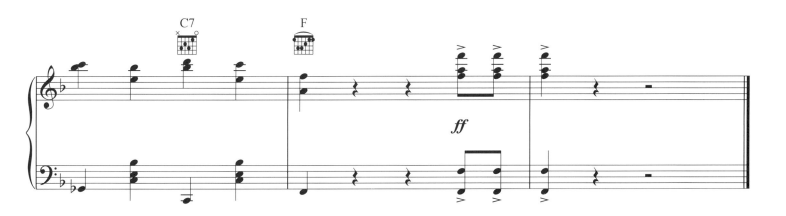

CHA-CHA

Music by
LEONARD BERNSTEIN

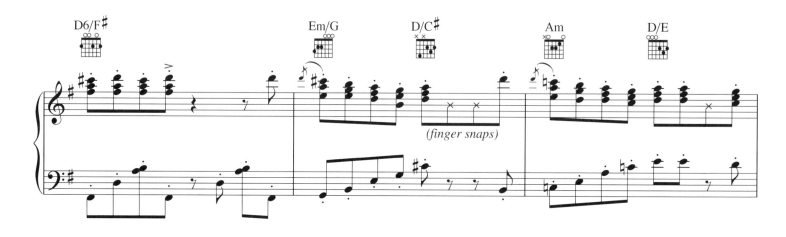
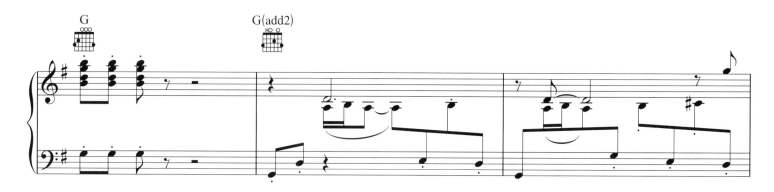

Copyright © 1957, 1959 by Amberson Holdings LLC and Stephen Sondheim
Copyright Renewed
This arrangement Copyright © 2007 by Amberson Holdings LLC and Stephen Sondheim
Leonard Bernstein Music Publishing Company LLC, Publisher
Boosey & Hawkes, Inc., Sole Agent
Copyright for All Countries. All Rights Reserved.

# TONIGHT

Music by LEONARD BERNSTEIN
Lyrics by STEPHEN SONDHEIM

The complete number, "Balcony Scene," is a duet for Maria and Tony, adapted here as a solo.

Copyright © 1957 by Amberson Holdings LLC and Stephen Sondheim
Copyright Renewed
This arrangement Copyright © 2007 by Amberson Holdings LLC and Stephen Sondheim
Leonard Bernstein Music Publishing Company LLC, Publisher
Boosey & Hawkes, Inc., Sole Agent
Copyright for All Countries. All Rights Reserved.

AMERICA

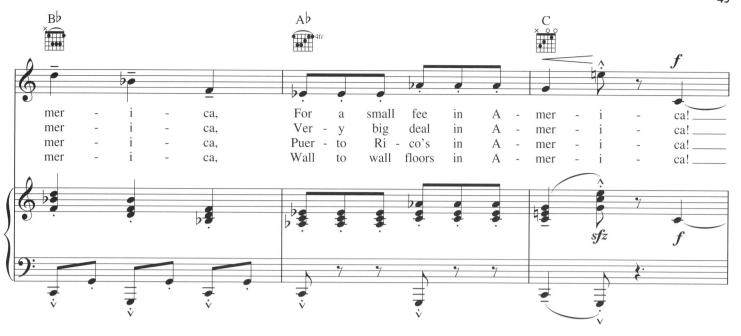
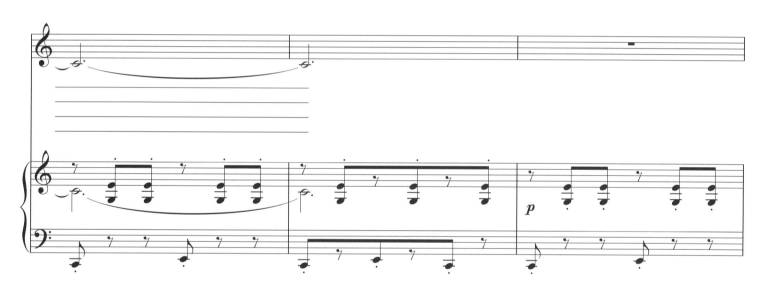
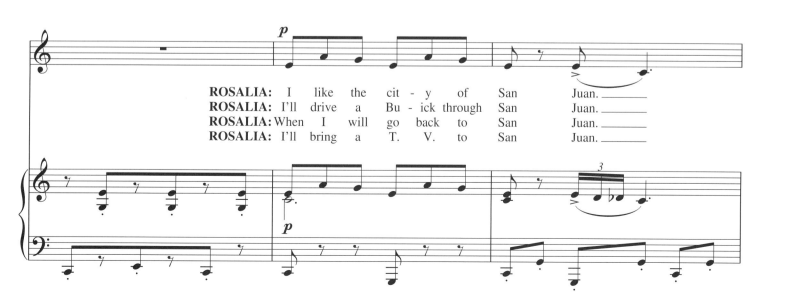

COOL

Music by LEONARD BERNSTEIN
Lyrics by STEPHEN SONDHEIM

ONE HAND, ONE HEART

Music by LEONARD BERNSTEIN
Lyrics by STEPHEN SONDHEIM

Originally a duet for Maria and Tony, adapted as a solo for this edition.

Copyright © 1957 by Amberson Holdings LLC and Stephen Sondheim
Copyright Renewed
This arrangement Copyright © 2007 by Amberson Holdings LLC and Stephen Sondheim
Leonard Bernstein Music Publishing Company LLC, Publisher
Boosey & Hawkes, Inc., Sole Agent
Copyright for All Countries. All Rights Reserved.

SOMEWHERE

Music by LEONARD BERNSTEIN
Lyrics by STEPHEN SONDHEIM

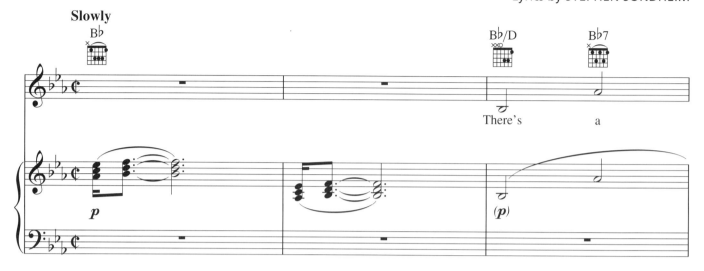

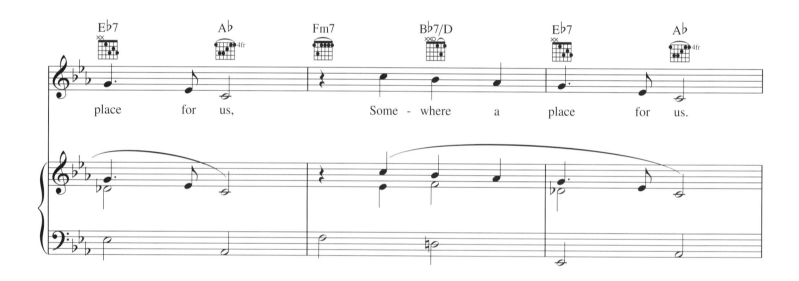

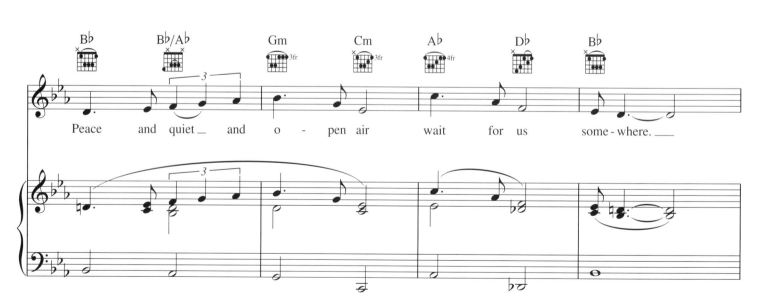

Copyright © 1957 by Amberson Holdings LLC and Stephen Sondheim
Copyright Renewed
This arrangement Copyright © 2007 by Amberson Holdings LLC and Stephen Sondheim
Leonard Bernstein Music Publishing Company LLC, Publisher
Boosey & Hawkes, Inc., Sole Agent
Copyright for All Countries. All Rights Reserved.

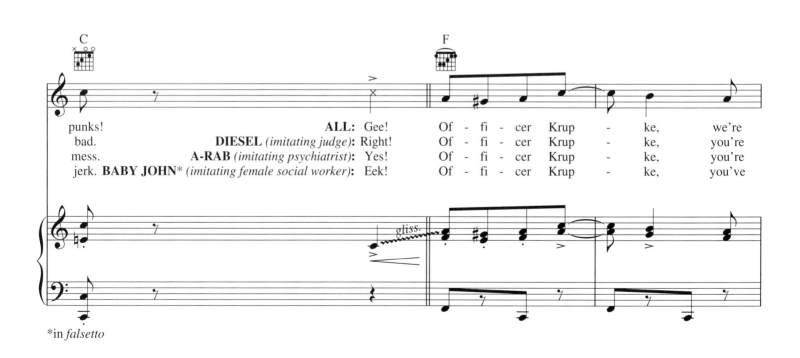

I HAVE A LOVE

Music by LEONARD BERNSTEIN
Lyrics by STEPHEN SONDHEIM

The complete number, "A Boy Like That/I Have a Love," is a duet for Anita and Maria, adapted as a solo for this edition.

Copyright © 1957, 1959 by Amberson Holdings LLC and Stephen Sondheim
Copyright Renewed
This arrangement Copyright © 2007 by Amberson Holdings LLC and Stephen Sondheim
Leonard Bernstein Music Publishing Company, Publisher
Boosey & Hawkes, Inc., Sole Agent
Copyright for All Countries. All Rights Reserved.

Facsimile from the composer's manuscript of "Cool."

Facsimile from the composer's manuscript of "I Feel Pretty."